PLAN THAT CAMPAIGN

LEARN EVERYTHING ABOUT CREATING WRITTEN MARKETING PLANS

ASHISH GUPTA

ISBN 979-888521404-9

Contents

CHAPTER ONE

WHAT IS MARKETING MASTERPLAN

Generally, marketers run ads hoping that enough people will respond and buy from them. However, we now understand that this is generally not the case. The ads can be run but without support infrastructure, these ads and the entire campaign may end up being ineffective.

We will learn to create a marketing system that will provide all the support infrastructure to your ads. It will provide the structure you need to run ads, generate leads, facilitate frequent communications to build trust, and finally sell the product. The system will also help you to sell repeatedly to the same buyer, and then create referrals and a word-of-mouth buzz.

Marketing is not a singular activity, it comprises a bunch of activities that together facilitate sales of a product. Good marketing requires proper planning and synchronization of each of these activities. Marketers tend to skip many of these activities or they may not allocate an appropriate amount of attention to some and therefore, they end up with broken campaigns.

This model is simple, tested, and quick for small business owners. We will try to make the process as objective as possible. It will make sure that the next marketing campaign you create is successful.

We will make sure that each step in your plan is effective. We will learn how to segment the market, research it, design a message, how to select channels, and so on. So let's get started with the process.

WHY DO YOU NEED MARKETING SYSTEMS?

If you do not have a marketing system in place, your marketing strategy would never be scalable. You would have scalability issues with your business as you would not be able to effectively market if the sales grow.

The problem with a lack of systems is that your entire team would not be certain about their respective roles. If you do not have a specific and well-defined system in place, your teammates will lose direction of the next course of action. It would hence lead to conflicted efforts by your teammates often leading to wastage of the company's resources. Not just your teammates, lack of a marketing system will also leave you unclear and ambiguous about the strategies, which will, in turn, lead to inconsistent efforts. You might be delivering different messages in each of your ads.

We know that it is very difficult to make the customer start believing in something. This is because the customer generally starts remembering anything only after he has seen it multiple times. So without consistency, your effort would not mean much. You have to be consistent to mean something to your prospects and to be consistent you need to have a full-fledged system in place.

Going forward we will design a full-fledged system. We will understand the different elements of a strategy and how to carry out each step involved in the process.

We will create a 'Marketing Masterplan' for each customer segment. Once that is in place, the main focus will shift from planning to executing the plan. Let us first see the 'Marketing Masterplan'.

CHAPTER TWO

MARKETING MASTERPLAN LAYOUT

WHY MARKETING MASTERPLAN?

We can see the Marketing Masterplan on the previous page. This page format breaks down the entire marketing exercise into smaller manageable chunks and once you plan for each of these parts, you will have a plan for the entire system. Most marketers go wrong because they start by thinking about the entire system as a whole without giving due attention to each individual block. It often leads to some blocks receiving way more attention while others not getting as much attention as they require.

It is only by thinking deeply about each individual building block can a person design a marketing strategy that has all the answers to problems that will arise in the marketing campaign. Also, such a systematic effort helps us exactly identify where are we going wrong in the marketing strategy and what is not working in the marketing campaign. Only after following such a holistic system, can a marketer be certain that the required infrastructure is in place.

Another mistake that many beginners make is that they only focus on the advertising stage in the marketing process. They tend to study the market and the product, design a message through an ad and then buy some media space to run the ads hoping that this would then directly lead to sales.

They underestimate the role of Trust Building Systems that are required to sustain the company in the long run. That is why we need to follow such a system-based Marketing Masterplan. It is very important to think clearly and actually implement the marketing campaign so as to achieve goals in the short run as well as the long run.

It is only by thinking deeply about each individual building block can a person design a marketing strategy

that has all the answers to problems that will arise in the marketing campaign.

Lorose

HOW DOES IT WORK

Notice that the entire Marketing Masterplan is broken down into smaller blocks and sub-blocks. We will learn about the activities to be performed in each block. We will understand how to strategize and plan for each block and then what skills are needed to execute them. If you plan and execute each block correctly, you will have a working marketing system in place.

How does it work? You have to first segment your total target market into smaller customer segments who are identical, have similar problems, etc. Once you identify your marketing segments, you have to create a Marketing Masterplan for each of these segments. So, let us say you want to sell a book and you could break the readers into 4 segments. Hence, you should create 4 'Marketing Masterplan', one for each segment. Only then you would have an exhaustive plan that can cater to the entire target market. However, do not forget the concept of 'Smallest Viable Market'.

Going forward we will learn how to segment the entire market and then we will understand each individual marketing activity that needs to be performed, what does each activity includes, and lastly how to implement the same. So let's get started with segmenting.

STEP 1: CUSTOMER SEGMENTATION

(A)

(B)

(C)
STEP 2: CREATE MASTERPLAN FOR EACH SEGMENT
Marketing Masterplan for (A)

Marketing Masterplan for (B)
Marketing Masterplan for (C)
OVERALL MARKETING SYSTEM

CHAPTER THREE

STEP 1: CUSTOMER SEGMENTATION

WHO
WHERE
WHAT
WHY
HOW

So the very first thing we need to do to create a marketing strategy is to segment the entire market into smaller parts. We have already understood the importance of a segmentation-based mindset in the 'Marketing mindset' module. It clearly describes why segmentation is important.

You know that people associate themselves with others who have similar traits i.e. they are "like them". If some people are like them, they not only think and behave in a similar manner but also communicate amongst themselves. This like-minded thinking and communication act as a benefit to the marketer.

The marketer must take advantage of this by identifying these groups of people who are similar in some or another way, and based on these similarities he should design a campaign that targets this smaller segment of people. So the offer design, message design, channel of communication, etc. can all be specific to this segment and can thus increase the chances of sales conversion. Imagine sending exactly the same communication to a doctor and lawyer for a product.

What are the chances of the message being very generic in nature? Very high. Similarly, what are the chances of the lead not converting to sales? Very high, right? Now you know why segmenting is important. It allows you to design a marketing strategy that is altered on the basis of the behavior of this particular market segment.

Now that we know what is segmenting and why it is so important, the next thing that becomes critical to learn is how to segment our market. Many marketers who know their market, do not segment it properly. They either segment based on factors that are not of utmost importance or they create segments that are too specific or too broad.

Failure to create proper market segments, failure to identify industries that are similar to each other lead to failure of the entire marketing plan.

The most important step to create proper segments is to identify the basis of dividing customer segments. We know that there can be hundreds of bases on which the market can be segmented. Also, two customers who belong to the same segment based on one parameter may at the same time belong to completely different segments based on another parameter.

So, the first step to identify customer segments is to identify the basis of segmentation of the market. The market can be segmented based on their geographical location, age group, profession, caste, gender, interests, and so on. It becomes almost impossible to list down all the bases, so we follow an interesting concept to segment the market.

We ask five questions and based on these questions we can segment the market. What are these questions? These questions include who, where, what, why and how. We will understand each one of them one by one.

WHO

The first basis of customer segmentation is 'who' the customer is. How the prospect identifies himself on different grounds can be used as a major basis for segmentation. For example, people of one gender think differently than others, people of one profession think differently than others, people of one caste think differently than others, etc. So people identify themselves differently than others and based on these 'who' factors different levels of customer segmentation can be carried out.

WHERE

The second basis for segmentation is 'where' i.e. where the customers are expected to buy the product, discover the product or use the product. Different geographical locations provide different living conditions and often determine the characteristics of the people living within that location. That is why segmentation based on 'where' plays a significant role.

WHAT

The next basis of segmentation is 'what' i.e. What does the prospect come to the company for? This is important particularly for companies that offer multiple products. For example, one might go to a supermarket for groceries whereas someone else might go for dairy products.

WHY

This refers to segmentation based on 'why' the customer wishes to buy the product or service. The motivation can be pains that will be relieved or gains that would be created. For example, someone might buy a car for transportation whereas someone else might buy it for social status.

Similarly, some people buy jewelry for consumption whereas others might buy it as an investment.

HOW

How the product would be used determines the segments in the market. The needs of someone who wants a laptop for gaming would be different from someone else who uses it to access basic MS office. The needs of those who use it daily would be different from those who use it once in a while.

EXAMPLES

WHO

- Gillette segments the market on the basis of gender. It has a different set of offerings for men and a completely different segment of offerings for Women.
- Media Houses segment their customers based on age groups. Based on these age groups, the media house runs different channels and produces different content. Political parties segment the electoral area based on caste or religion.
- Segments for a Finance book may include CA students, MBA students, and investors. Restaurants segment based on tastes of its consumers. So different cuisines would be introduced based on what people from different cultures want to eat.
- Recruiters segment potential employees on the basis of education and experience.

WHERE

- Clothing companies segment the market on the basis of their geography. The material used is decided on the basis of 'where' the product will be used. Architects make construction designed based on 'where' the construction is to be done i.e. considering factors like topography, climate, etc.
- Film Makers segment the market based on 'where' when making regional content

WHAT

- BigBazaar can segment its market based on those who come for groceries, those for clothes, those for electronics, and so on.
- Croma segments its customers based on those who come for home appliances and those who come for office appliances. Byju's can segment its customers based on those who come for K-12 classes and those who come for higher education

WHY

- Almost all goods bought for social benefits have a 'why' segment to them. You might buy a house, car, or clothes for its utility function or for its social benefit.

HOW

- Mobile phone companies segment their users based on 'how'. Some users use phones for calling, others for photography, some others for media consumption, etc. So how the product would be used determines the market segment.

CHAPTER FOUR

STEP 2: CREATING MARKETING SYSTEM

Once the market has been segmented, the next step to be taken is to create a marketing system or marketing plan for each of these segments. As we saw the 'Marketing Masterplan' earlier, we need to create a similar plan for each of the target market. But where do you start from?

Once you have segmented the market, you need to select which is the best segment for you to serve. You can even serve multiple segments. Remember, larger the market, higher the probability of scaling up. But on the other side, larger the market, larger the risk of not meeting needs and wants of any particular group. Also it means, higher would be cost incurred to serve these markets. So a balance must be achieved. Recall the reading that described the 'Minimum Viable Concept'.

Once you have identified the target markets, we would create a one pager for each segment. This would require a lot of brainstorming. Another important source of ideas would be learning from others. What others have done and has worked for them? Some of the greatest marketing campaigns have borrowed a lot from other campaigns. Use various sources to create a marketing system.

Going forward we will explain the marketing system or the 'Marketing Masterplan'. The 5 activities of the Marketing Masterplan are referred as blocks, we will explain how each activity is to be performed. We will discuss what are the important checklists or models that you need to use.

Once you do this for each segment, you would have a plan that is complete and should sell your product if the value proposition is decently strong. So let us begin with understanding the marketing system.

CHAPTER FIVE

BLOCK 1: RESEARCH

The very first step after segmenting the customers and deciding which ones to serve is to carry out an in-depth research of the target market. This is to be done for each individual customer segment. You need to understand the customers on different grounds i.e. customer's thoughts, purchase behavior, consumption behavior about the product and so on.

Based on these we will identify the message that can be drafted for the customer in each communication. This will help us establish a better rapport with the customer. This will also help us create marketing collaterals that appeal more to the customer.

Explorer, thrives for adventures

Marketing experts have a common saying amongst them – "Research shows and sells." This means that it is essential for companies to research the market and it shows in the marketing campaign whether or not the designer of the campaign has studied the customer properly. It also indicates whether he understands the customer or not.

Not only this, good customer research also gets the results required by the marketer. Because marketing content created with the support of good customer research creates more attention, interest and desire, it ends up selling more. A proper system to research the market is a must for any marketer. That is why, we often see a single person successfully creating ads across different industries i.e.

because he carries out an in-depth customer research.

Intellectual, informed and educated

Going forward, we will learn how to conduct proper market research. We will understand in further parts of the course, what models to use to conduct market research and what methods can we use to get the required data.

Leader, hardworking and achievers

CHAPTER SIX

ARROW: MESSAGE TO TARGET MARKET

The Bridge between research and the channel to be used is - Message to the market. Once you have segmented the market and carried out in-depth research about each of these customer segments, their buying patterns, consumption patterns, etc. you need to design and draft a message for your customers. You have to decide what is it that you would want to convey to them. But here is a challenge.

According to your research, you would find multiple things that influence the sales of your offerings and you would want to address all of them. But the problem is you cannot address all the issues. You cannot say all that you want to. No one will give you that much attention. So, you will have to decide which is the most important message that you want to convey and based on this get the attention and interest of the prospects.

Drafting the message becomes a huge challenge because you have to say a limited number of things in a limited frame and in a way that appeals to the prospect. Many marketers may not be able to clearly decide on what message they want to give to the market and they may end up giving multiple messages in the same marketing piece.

This counts for a huge mistake as you cannot expect the prospect to remember so many things about you. The interest of prospects cannot be demanded, instead, it has to be earned. This can be done by regularly conveying messages that they want to hear.

Recall the concept of 'focus' that we discussed earlier. As an extension to that remembers that for all marketing communications – Clarity is the key.

GROUND RULES FOR DELIVERING A GOOD MESSAGE

First, you can only communicate with the market, if you have done proper research. So, do not skip the research stage. Nor should you rush in that step as important insights would go unnoticed.

Next, for all communications, clarity is the key. Decide properly on what you want to say and when. Focus on that only. You can communicate more in detail once the person shows some interest. But do not try to tell everything here. Just focus on the most important messages i.e. focus on those messages that will get the customer interested. Say what you want to and nothing else. For example, if you are talking about a habit of your customer, just show that habit and nothing else. Do not try to tell a few other habits too.

Also, all messages should be created in a way such that they are customer-centric. The customer is not interested in you or your product but himself. Tell him what the product will do for him. Tell him how will it impact his life. Tell him how will things change for him going forward. Tell him about himself. Be customer-centric as we discussed earlier.

Make sure that you tell him why is the customer better off buying from you and not your competition. At most places, your communication should focus on your differentiation factor or your Unique Selling Proposition (USP) and how it will improve the customer's life.

While delivering a message to the market, remember the phrase – Show, don't tell. If you can show something to the prospect, the impact will be much more than just telling your prospect about it. Also, while deciding on the message, work with a 'Proof mindset'. Do not make 3-4 claims and leave them. Instead, make a singular claim and focus on its proof. A single item proved is better than multiple items simply claimed.

Many times, the most important piece of communication would be your offer. You may, at times, believe that your offer is so good that the prospect would show interest solely based on the offer. In such cases, you should communicate the offer itself. But, when you are communicating the offer directly, keep in mind that you are beginning with hard selling and not going through a soft selling route.

Whenever you communicate the offer directly, you should communicate all three things – Value, Bonus, and Guarantee. Make sure you communicate the exchange value which indicates the benefits that the buyer receives against the value he pays. Next, give a bonus to the prospect. Something he did not expect. You may give him some benefit to delight him prior to purchase.

Lastly, show him that your claims are true i.e. give him a guarantee by reducing the risk in his purchase. You can do this by giving a free trial, a free demo, a money-back guarantee, etc. All these things together reduce the risk and help to get the prospect interested.

HOW TO DRAFT A MESSAGE

Here we have to understand what needs to be done to draft an effective message. Remember, drafting a message is an art as well as a science. It has some fixed rules that you have to follow but at the same time, it also has an artistic and creative side to it. The most important thing that you need to do is to research the market, as discussed earlier.

If you research the market properly, most of your questions would be answered. If you research the market segments properly, you would automatically figure out what to say to the market and when to say it. Going forward, we shall discuss market research.

Once you have decided what is to be said, next, you need to decide – How to say it? For this, you need two major skills. These are copywriting and advertisement creation. At this stage, you can either hire an outsider to take care of this step, or smaller business owners who are short on resources can begin doing it themselves.

First, let us understand what copywriting is. Copywriting is basically selecting words to convey the message such that it is catchy and generates interest. In a way, it is glossing the message to make it more effective. Copywriting is all about words. What words you select for an ad, email, brochure, etc. determine its attractiveness. This is what a copywriter does.

Next, you need to learn how great ads are created. Remember, we already discussed how creativity is best stolen. We will learn how we can create great ads for ourselves at very low budgets going forward. For now, keep in mind the process. First, you need to research and decide what to say and then you also need to decide how to say it. We will do that when we learn how to write copies and get ad ideas.

What words you select for an ad, email, brochure etc. determine its attractiveness. This is what copywriter does.

The last thing that needs to be done is to create a proof for your communication. For this, we will learn various proof techniques. We will also learn how to manage public relations at a very low budget.

If we can create an attractive message and deliver it properly, the marketing campaign's results go up manifold. The reason behind this is whatever you communicate at this stage will form your first impression in the minds of the buyer and a first impression is very important as people make snap judgments.

They do not think consciously about your ads or your message. They just see something and judge it subconsciously i.e. good or bad. Judgments about you are made in less than 3 seconds. So be very careful about what you say and how you say it for the first time.

EXAMPLES OF CLEAR MESSAGE
1
Healthy teeth with
Colgate

m om
m usic
m oney
m iracle
Everything great starts with "M"
2
m&m's

adidas
YOU ARE
#NEVERDONE
THE TIME, THE HUSTLE - YOU KEEP PUSHING THROUGH YOUR LIMITS.
FOR YOU WHO KNOWS NO BOUNDARIES.
@ADIDASWOMEN RANGE NOW AVAILABLE AT lifestyle
3

CHAPTER SEVEN

BLOCK 2: CHANNELS TO USE

Once you have decided, what to say and how to say it, the next question that arises is where to say it? For this, you have to decide what channels you want to use to convey your message. For example, you may use traditional channels such as newspapers, radio, TV, etc. or you may use digital channels of today. For most small business owners, digital channels play a key role as they can start advertising at very low budgets.

Many companies also use new and/or innovative channels to deliver their message. For example, some advertise on airports, buses, cars, pavements, beaches and many more. Some other companies take it a level up, with being more innovative and engaging by using guerrilla marketing techniques. Guerrilla marketing means advertising in hidden places where the prospect does not expect.

But once he sees that ad, he is rather surprised and because he is surprised, more often than not, he remembers you and your message. The way to find new and innovative places where small business owners can advertise again lies in research.

You have to understand how the prospect spends most of his day, what he does, where he goes, what all are his surroundings, and based on that decide where you can possibly get your ad or message delivered. Identifying new channels is not as easy as it sounds but if you can find few innovative channels, you would be able to deliver your message in a much cheaper and much more effective way.

Basically, any place where the prospects spend their time and you can get a message delivered, you can use it as a channel. For example, Ola used boats to help people caught in Chennai floods and then used it to advertise saying – "Whatever happens, we are available for your transport." A large number of such techniques can be used to create guerrilla marketing campaigns. Remember that new channels that are not well discovered as an ad medium are under-priced because they are still trying to attract marketers.

In the later stage, we will learn about Guerrilla marketing. We will explore more of the website called - www.themediaant.com which offers great data about the available channels for advertisement. What you can also do is constantly be on the lookout for new apps in the market that are launching their own ad networks – such as Hotstar, Inshorts, Yourstory, etc. All these companies, in their initial years, try to attract advertisers, and hence they are relatively under-priced.

YOURSTORY

However, be very careful about the media through which you are advertising. Getting your message across is the key but you also need to understand that snap judgment are made about you using the media platform to target people. For example, companies that advertise on platforms such as Tiktok because the ad rates are cheaper, tend to be interpreted as a mass-market product.

Now, if a product that is a little more upmarket and intellectual in nature, such as this course, starts advertising on Tiktok, the course would not make a very good first impression. So, marketers need to be very careful about how they use of channels of communication is interpreted.

Do not consider 'inexpensive' as the only parameter to judge the effectiveness of a channel. You need quality in reach much more than you need quantity. It is of no use if 10,000 people see your ad but none form part of your market. Instead, it is much better to advertise to only 100 who are directly interested in your topic.

While selecting the channel, focus on quality more than quantity. To have proper answers to where most of your market spends time, you need to research the market in much more detail. Also, remember that whatever media you use to advertise, you must invest time to learn more about that particular media. For example, if you want to advertise through social media, you must learn the basics of social media marketing.

Also, know that consumer behavior keeps on changing. So you must keep on changing the channel as people move from one medium to another.

EXAMPLES OF GUERRILLA MARKETING

Sprite
REFRESQUE
SUAS IDEIAS
Sprite
Sprite
Sprite
2

USE ONLY
WHAT YOU
NEED.
DENVER WATER
3

Mars
TRUCK SIZE
4

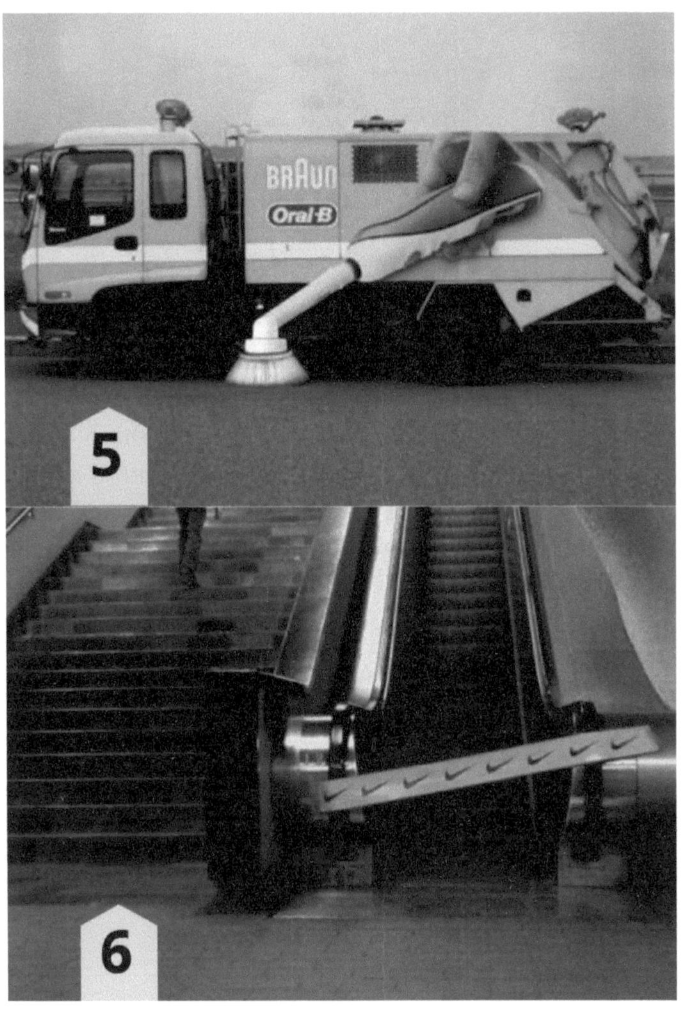
BRAUN
Oral-B
5
6

CHAPTER EIGHT

BLOCK 3: TRUST BUILDING SYSTEM

How often does it happen that we buy from those whom we do not trust? Not very often, right? The truth is people will say all things to you, but not buy from you until they trust you. Guess why do you buy from Apple, Samsung, or even your local Kirana store. They will give you what is promised i.e. you trust them. Similarly, it is important for all marketers to build trust and have a system for it.

Now, the process is simple to understand, yet difficult to execute. Based on the ads that you run, some people will take the action that you asked them to i.e. call a number, fill a form, sign up, visit a store, etc. By taking this they are giving you the 'permission' to contact them. These people - the ones who take action - are indirectly saying that they are interested in your offering.

However, they are not ready to buy as yet. These are what we call 'leads'. You need to have a full-fledged system for building trust with them. Remember, they will not buy from you unless they trust you. So, a trust-building system is essential.

Many marketers go wrong when they advertise to directly sell rather than advertising to generate leads. Advertising to selling works if the prospect already knows you and trusts you. But if he does not know you and trust you, then you have to advertise to capture the lead and then nurture it over time before selling.

Remember, the rule is – "Do not sell before the prospect trusts you." If you try selling before building trust, not only will the customer not buy from you but also, your entire marketing effort will fail.

WAYS TO BUILD TRUST

We already discussed what are some important strategies used to build trust in the first book. There are other ways to do it as well. These include tie-ups, affiliations, endorsements, etc. All these help the prospect gain trust over the company and its offering. Remember, when it comes to trust-building, money is in the follow-up. That means how you follow up on your prior communication determines a lot about your marketing success.

You must have a clear communication strategy ready about how and when will you communicate with the leads. You can have a strategy in place for daily, weekly, monthly, quarterly, and yearly communication. Now, if you are a small firm or a single-person firm, you can decide and have a weekly and monthly strategy in place. But always remember, in marketing, money is always in the follow-up.

If you do not ask, you will not get it.

It is not the prospect's job to remember when is the next review deadline. It is your job to remember when was his response due and then remind him to respond if he hasn't already.

Once you have a communication strategy in place, next you need to decide what medium you would select to deliver the message. You could send it over emails, over messages, over Whatsapp, through app notifications, or even physically using a letter, a postcard, a gift, etc.

Be careful about the medium you use as it will again decide what impression you form. Going forward, we will see what different communication strategies you can build.

You can also build trust through content marketing. That means creating content on your subject and then distributing it on social media channels. This helps gain a lot of trust as you appear to have authority over the subject.

We will see how content creation can be done going forward and we will also see how some of the most successful content marketers distribute their content. We will content model about how the entire process can be speeded up. We will also see how PR is one of the most effective ways to build trust in our book 'Public Relations'.

We saw the importance of follow-ups. Now, orchestrate few initial interactions, and then based on what the prospect says or does, you can create a follow-up infrastructure. Now, this becomes very tedious and almost impossible for one man to do on his own. Also, most of it is very repetitive. So what can do is, you can put in place a

Customer Relationship Manager i.e. CRM software in place. The content strategy that you have made can also be run on this CRM system.

CRM system automates most of the communication such that the human interaction with the prospect is possible only when there is a need. We will learn more about CRM and its use in trust-building process going forward.

Another important way to build trust and nurture leads is by offering value before purchase. This can be accomplished by a free trial, by providing educative content, etc. You can also consult with your prospects and try and solve their problems. All this gets him to trust you and the lead slowly and steadily moves closer to sales.

So, we see that we need to have a content strategy, a communication strategy, a follow-up infrastructure, and lastly a CRM in place. All these together shall build enough trust in the minds of the prospects. We will understand each of them going forward. But know that, all these are inter-related. Only after the lead has started to trust us, can we move them to the sales stage. This stage involves an exchange of values between the two parties.

The customer pays the amount in exchange for the value promised by the marketer. The key here is to adequately judge whether or not a lead is ready for sales. If you start selling before he trusts you, the lead would go away and all effort would be wasted and if you sell too late, he would buy elsewhere. The way to identify this is by pushing soft offers once in while and checking his interest.

If he responds with intent, you can move him to sales else, he will spend more time in the nurturing phase.

TRUST BUILDING FLOW: EXAMPLE

Day from inquiry	Message	Medium
1	Thank you for your inquiry	Phone
7	Research report relevant to request at inquiry	Email
30	Case study of success from company in inquirer's industry	Email
45	Seminar invitation	Phone
60	Customer testimonial and personalized letter	Mail
75	Link to article from trade journal	Email
90	Personal note from sales engineer to schedule online demo	Email
105	White paper and personal cover letter	Mail
125	Invitation to breakfast seminar at trade show	Email

Credits: ruthstevens.com

EXAMPLE OF TRUST BUILDING SYSTEM

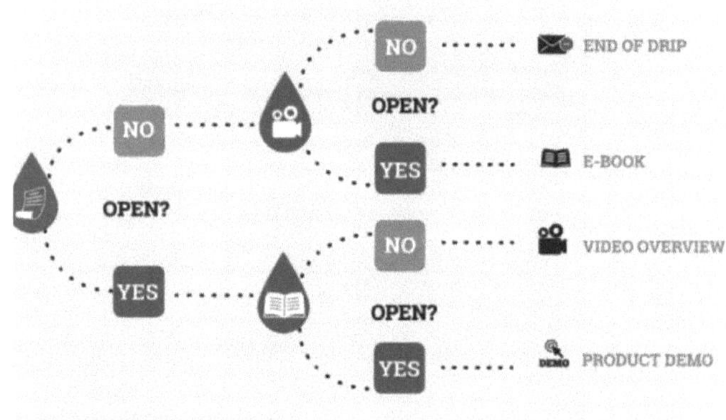

Credits: engagebay.com

CHAPTER NINE

BLOCK 4: SALES CONVERSION STRATEGY

> ***Every sale has five basic obstacles: no need, no money, no hurry, no desire, no trust.***
>
> ***Zig Ziglar***

Once the prospect or the lead has begun to trust us, we can move over to sales. Sales is the step where you ask the prospect to buy something from you. You ask him to take action and buy something from you. This is the step where you make your profits. But the problem is marketers often get too excited and start selling too early. Marketers who sell too early cause their prospects to turn away. They have a difficult time building the trust with the prospect because the prospect ends up thinking that the marketer is only interested in himself.

On the other hand, some marketers start selling too late and in the meanwhile risk their prospects being chased by the competitors. That is why it becomes very important to time the purchases of the prospects. You get cold leads, you build trust with them and when you think they trust you, you try and sell to them. Timing is one of the important factors in drafting sales strategy.

In many cases, despite timing the sale properly, the marketers may end up not meeting their sales expectations. The reason for this is an improper sales conversion strategy. Remember, if you do everything well but stop at the sales conversion strategy, your marketing system becomes unsustainable. The reason for this is that sales is the stage where marketing systems generate cash to fund the entire system. Remember, "Sales Cure it All". This stage tests how well have you executed all the other steps.

> ***You are not trying to convince them of anything. You are trying to show them how you are going to make their lives easier... There are no favors involved. It's a win-win for everybody. Every no gets you closer to a yes. It's a numbers game...***
>
> ***It's just a question of making calls.***

Mark Cuban

Lorose

HOW TO CONVERT TO SALES

One of the biggest pitfalls in sales is that marketers rely too much on hope. If you have a well-thought-out marketing strategy, this step would also fall in place. You have to actively think and fix all the steps that are not working in the marketing strategy. Only after this will you be in a position where leads will convert to sales. You cannot leave any step to luck and hope. You have to actively plan for it.

One of the most tried and tested methods to build trust is educating the prospect. Educate, educate and educate till the time the prospect gets to trust you. This is done at the trust-building stage.

Another model that helps build trust is advisory-based selling. Marketers shall act as advisors or counselors to the prospects and help them solve their problems. Once they know the solution of a problem, they will most likely hire you to solve it for them. That means they will end up buying your product or service. This generally works great in a B2B business.

Another important factor is to focus on 'Risk Reduction'. That means every time a prospect buys something, he is entering into unknown territory. He does not know what to expect from the company. He is only buying based on your promise but he still has risks. So, whenever selling, try to reduce the risk as much as possible. The reason for this is that he wants to know what to expect after buying the product. That is why it is easier to sell to repeat buyers. They know what they can expect from the product/ company.

So all the selling should focus on reducing customer's risks. The way out is 'communication'. Research the market and address the common concerns that prospects have even before they ask you. This gives an impression to the customer that the company understands him and cares about him. Address all his fears and concerns.

Another method to reduce risks is by giving an outrageous guarantee. Give the prospect a guarantee such that it reduces his risk in the purchase. This will incentivize him to go ahead with the transaction. Tools like money-back guarantee, free trial, guaranteed results, compensation tied to performance, etc. can be used to get him to trust you.

The offer also plays a critical role in the selling activity. Make sure that your offer is very attractive. Design an offer that acts as a catalyst in the sales process. Make sure that you offer enough value in exchange for what you are asking. While designing the offer, try being in the shoes of the prospect as much as possible.

Also, make it easy for the prospect to buy. You need to make the process simple and hold his hand at every step with appropriate communication so that he walks through the entire process and ends up buying your product or service.

If the above-said things are taken care of, generally your

leads would convert to sales. Remember, you do not want to keep selling all the time. But you have to sell at the time it is required. You do not want to leave sales to luck. Also remember, selling is the only stage where you are asking something from the prospect. People will drop out of the process at this stage. Rejection is a part of the process. So do not get disheartened by it. You only need few people to buy for your marketing funnel to succeed.

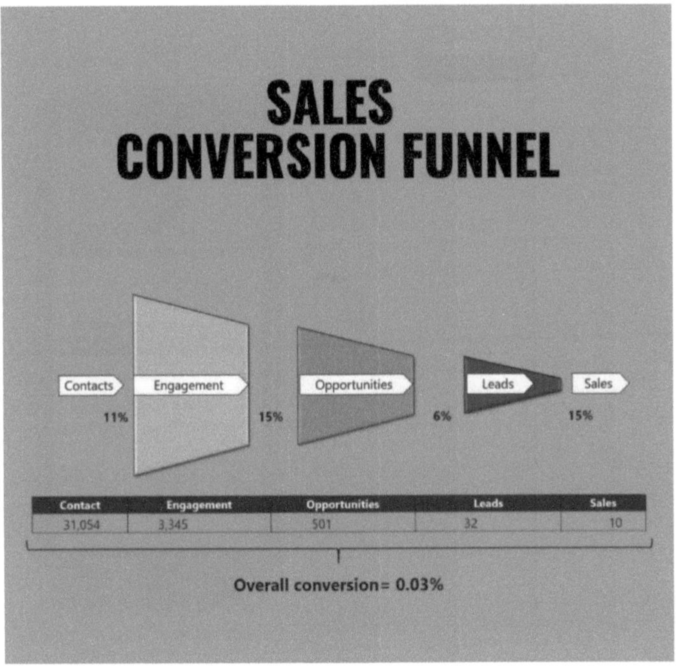

HARD SALES TECHNIQUES

You can see how the firm is reducing risks by offering a buyback guarantee.

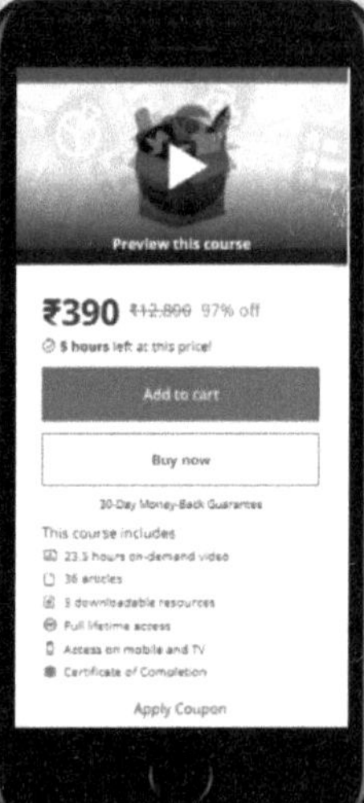

Notice how the firm is using hard selling concepts. It is creating a sense of urgency, elaborating an offer. Also the firm is reducing risk by giving a 30-Day Money-Back Guarantee.

CHAPTER TEN

BLOCK 5: GETTING PEOPLE TO TALK

The last step to create a complete marketing system is to develop a system to generate referrals and feedback. Many marketers may feel that this is not important and does not determine the success of any marketing campaign. Well, the truth is, it has the ability to reduce your marketing costs drastically. This stage of marketing is cheap and very effective.

One challenge advertisement is, people do not trust something when they hear from advertisers. On the other hand, they trust it when they hear the same thing from their friends i.e. through word-of-mouth. Word-of-mouth has a huge power to convert leads to sales because trust is already established. So, marketers need to work consciously on creating word-of-mouth value for their products.

Sometimes the easiest way to get word-of-mouth is to ask people to tell their friends about it. Because it is so basic and easy, most marketers think it won't work. However, if you honestly call up your customers, ask them about their customer experience and ask them to refer to their friends if the answer is positive, this itself would generate a lot of referrals. So one of the simplest strategies is to ask people to refer you to someone else.

Honest follow-up and genuinely showing interest in people go a long way. If you care about your customers and they know it, they will care about you too.

The next strategy to create buzz is by constantly creating content that is 'Shareable'. If you create content that genuinely interests the customer, he will share it with his friends. And because of that, you would get to reach many more people. Going forward we will see how to create such content.

Another way to interact with your customers and prospects from a position of trust is by contracting businesses that the prospect already buys from. The prospect buys from them because he trusts them and believes in whatever the business has to say. So another way to get referrals is by contacting other businesses that sell something else but to the same set of customers.

The next approach that can be used is to create gift cards and vouchers. So whenever an existing customer shares that with any new prospect, both of them benefit. In this way, you too get new business. This is one of the most common methods used by startups to scale. However, this generally leads to cash burn as expenses go up.

Another form of referral-based marketing is Affiliate Marketing. Affiliate marketing is when a person in a position of influencing affiliates to sell your products, and every time he sells it, he takes a commission from the sale. Affiliates help expand the reach of the product to new audiences.

The above mentioned are some of the common methods that are used to make people talk. However, these are methods that incentivize people to refer to your products as a business, these do not inspire common people to talk about your product. Only when people talk about your product, business on their own, will news spread like fire. This can be done by having 'hooks' in your product or marketing. 'Hooks' are those features or topics that are talked about by people i.e. they deserve word-of-mouth.

EXAMPLES OF REFER & EARN

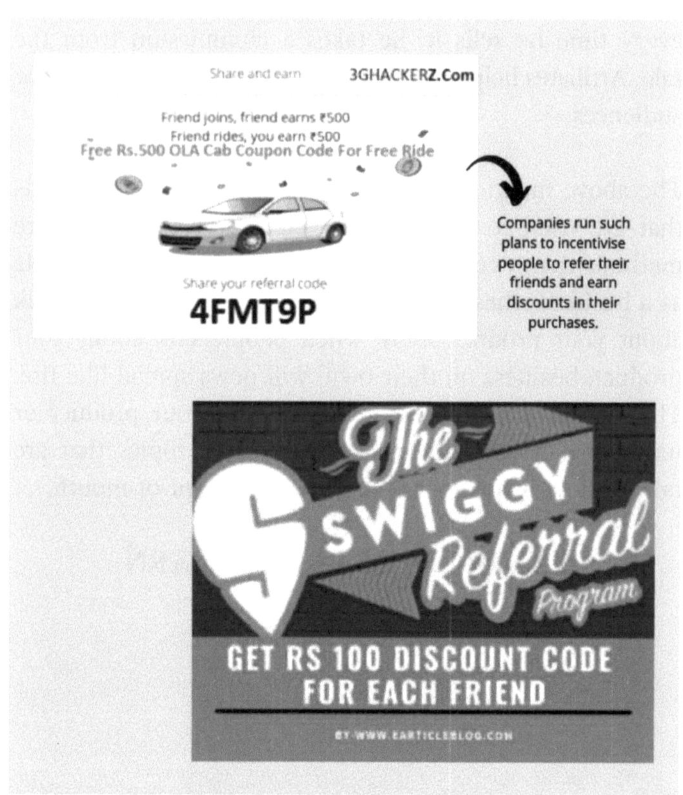

EXAMPLES OF REFERRALS

amazon India
associates
Affiliate Program
Start Making Money With
Amazon.in Affiliate Program
These are examples of affiliate marketing by Amazon and tie-ups between two firms to refer customers to each other so that they can mutually benefit.
kotak
Everyday Specials
bigbasket
10%
instant discount
kotak
Everyday Specials
PVR
Buy One,
Get One Free

CHAPTER ELEVEN

CONCLUSION

Now you know how the entire system works. You know each element of the 'Marketing Masterplan'. You need to create a system where a person enters and goes through the loop multiple times. Only then can we create repeat sales. All marketers need to design such a system for each of their customer segments. That means if a product has 4 market segments, then 4 such sheets would be created. But once you have created such a sheet, you would be able to get the entire team on the same page.

Once you have planned, the next challenge remains in execution. So this plan can act as a strong foundation for your execution. If you create such a complete plan for each segment for each product in your business, you will have a complete marketing system in place.

Remember, you will not get the entire system right at the first go. You will create a system, where people would get stuck at different stages. You will then make changes to help people walk through the process. This is how the system is created over time. Up to this stage, we have learned how this system looks like.

Now, we would learn the different skills required to carry out this activity even if your team is small. We will learn the tricks and techniques to carry out each activity. Going forward we will cover them one by one in further books.

SKILLS AND CONCEPTS YOU NEED TO KNOW

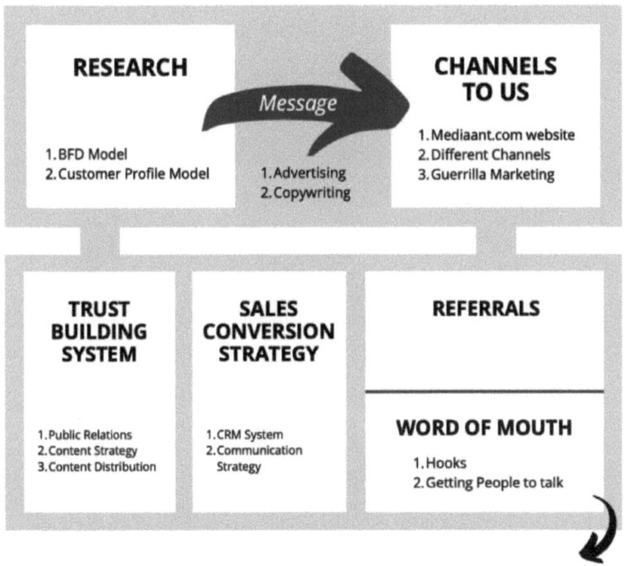

Going forward we will understand each of them one by one so that not only are you able to design a system, but also implement it completely, even if you are a solo entrepreneur. Remember, all these topics are a matter of practice. You will not be able to perform them as well as a professional. But you will do enough good to take care of your marketing till the time you do not become large to afford professionals.

Printed by Libri Plureos GmbH in Hamburg,
Germany